The complete unit guide for the Certificate in Education and Training

Understanding Roles, Responsibilities and Relationships in Education and Training

Nabeel Zaidi

LLB (Hons), LLM, Pg.Dip. DMS, MBA, Cert. Ed., Barrister

Copyright © Nabeel Zaidi, 2015

First edition published in 2015

The moral right of Nabeel Zaidi to be identified as the author of this work has been asserted by him in accordance with the Copyright, Designs and Patents Act 1988.

All rights reserved. No part of this publication may be reproduced, stored in a retrieval system, or transmitted in any form or by any means, electronic, mechanical, photocopying, recording, or otherwise, without the prior permission of the copyright owner of this book.

About this book

This textbook provides the information and guidance needed to pass the unit. It is written for all awarding organisations and focuses on each of the learning outcomes and assessment criteria of the unit. Detailed explanation is given, together with supporting examples and links to various other resources, which will be useful to those about to enter a teaching or training role or those newly appointed to such a role. Detailed guidance is also provided on structuring responses to meet the requirements of unit assessment criteria. This textbook considers multiple perspectives relevant to teaching, training, assessing, tutoring, quality assurance and educational management.

About the author

Nabeel has been in the further education sector since 1996, occupying various lecturing, middle and senior management and consultancy roles, including working with several awarding organisations, undertaking quality assurance assignments, delivering professional training to the education sector on equality and diversity and the Ofsted common inspection framework and developing and delivering on undergraduate and post-graduate business management programmes and teaching qualifications. He is also a Reviewer for the Quality Assurance Agency (QAA) and runs his own college and consultancy company.

Nabeel holds various academic and professional qualifications and titles, including being a qualified Barrister, an MBA in Educational Management (University of Leicester), a Certificate in Education (Institute of Education), a Post-Graduate Diploma in Professional Legal Skills (Inns of Court School of Law / City University), a Master's degree in Law (University College London), a degree in Law (Queen Mary's College, University of London), and a Post-Graduate Diploma in Management Studies.

Contents

Introduction 6

The teaching role and responsibilities in education and training 6

1. The teaching role and responsibilities in education and training 6

    (a) Lecturer..6

    (b) Trainer 7

    (c) Tutor 8

    (d) Assessor..8

2. Key aspects of legislation and regulatory requirements relevant to the teaching role 10

    (a) Key legislation 10

    (b) Regulatory requirements..15

3. Promoting equality and valuing diversity 16

    (a) Equality Act 2010 and Ofsted...16

    (b) Learning disabilities, difficulties and medical conditions 18

    (c) Reducing other barriers to learning 18

4. Identifying and meeting individual learner needs 19

Ways to maintain a safe and supportive learning environment 21

1. Maintaining a safe and supportive learning environment 21

    (a) Safe physical environment...21

    (b) Supportive learning environment......................................22

        (i) Ground rules at the beginning of the programme 22

        (ii) Ground rules at the beginning of a session or before an activity .22

        (iii) Negotiating ground rules 22

    (c) Structured learning environment.......................................23

    (d) Individual support 23

    (e) Pair work and group work 24

2. Promoting appropriate behaviour and respect for others 24

    (a) Policies and procedures...24

    (b) Learner contracts 25

(c) Inclusive learning environment and learning resources..................25

The relationships between teachers and other professionals in education and training **27**

1. Working with other professionals...27

(a) Planning 27

(b) Sharing assessment outcomes / learner progress 27

(c) Communicating learner needs 28

(d) Negotiating support for learners 28

(e) Contributing to internal quality assurance 29

(f) Liaising with referral agencies 30

2. The boundaries between the teaching role and other professional roles 30

(a) Personal boundaries..30

(b) Professional boundaries 31

3. Points of referral to meet individual learner needs 31

(a) Organisation systems and procedures 31

(b) External agencies 32

Command verbs (used in this unit) 33

Glossary of key terms used in this textbook..34

STRUCTURING EFFECTIVE RESPONSES TO MEET THE REQUIREMENTS OF THE UNIT **39**

Understanding the bigger picture..40

Understanding Roles, Responsibilities and Relationships in Education and Training **42**

Assessment criterion 1.1 43

Assessment criterion 1.2 44

Assessment criterion 1.3 46

Assessment criterion 1.4 48

Assessment criterion 2.1 49

Assessment criterion 2.2 50

Assessment criterion 3.1 52

Assessment criterion 3.2 53

Assessment criterion 3.3 54

Introduction

Understanding Roles, Responsibilities and Relationships in Education and Training is a mandatory unit of the *Certificate in Education and Training*. The purpose of this textbook is to provide candidates with the underpinning content to meet the assessment criteria of the unit.

Definition of roles for the purposes of this textbook:

Role	Definition
Lecturer/Teacher/ Trainer/Tutor/Assessor	the person taking the Certificate in Education and Training qualification.
Learner/Student	the person being taught or assessed by the Lecturer/ Teacher/Trainer/Tutor/Assessor.
CET Tutor	the person delivering/facilitating the Certificate in Education and Training qualification.

The teaching role and responsibilities in education and training

1. The teaching role and responsibilities in education and training

(a) Lecturer

Lecturers normally work in Further Education colleges, higher education institutions and private colleges. The extent of the role can be very prescriptive or very wide ranging, with additional responsibilities, depending on the size, type or ethos of the organisation. That aside, there are some common elements. These can include planning, preparing and delivering part of a course or the entire course, contributing towards quality assurance, adhering to organisation policies and procedures and awarding organisation requirements (typical awarding organisations include Pearson, AQA, OCR, City and Guilds).

Planning can include preparing and/or delivering to schemes of work. These outline the unit content of a course to be delivered per week or per session, the assessment objectives being applied, assessment methods and resources to be used and differentiation strategies for each session. Lecturers may also complete lesson plans, which provide more detailed information about the lesson aim(s), lesson objectives, how lesson objectives are going to be assessed, the content to be covered and the teaching, learning and differentiation strategies to be applied.

Where internally assessed courses are being delivered, lecturers may also be expected to design assignment briefs / assessment instruments and internally verify each other's assignment briefs before they are issued. Assignment briefs include a set of tasks that learners are required to complete to pass part of or the entire unit. Internal verification includes a set of checks that a colleague lecturer (who may or may not be a qualified internal verifier) undertakes to make sure that the assignment brief or assessment instrument is fit for purpose (i.e. it is capable of generating valid, reliable and timely evidence and outcomes).

Lecturers are expected to be familiar with key organisation policies and procedures, especially those relevant to their role. These can include policies and procedures relating to health and safety, equality and diversity, safeguarding, assessment and internal verification, examinations, invigilation, teaching and learning, assessment malpractice and maladministration, conflict of interest, learner discipline and gifts and bribes. Lecturers tend to disseminate information through lectures, presentations, discussions, facilitation of group work and leading on external visits.

(b) Trainer

Depending on the context, the role of a trainer is normally more versatile than that of a lecturer, often focusing on skills building, presenting complex information in a short timeframe, actively / frequently facilitating team and group working, having a more practical dimension to sessions (e.g. demonstrating techniques) and being more vocationally focused. Trainers often deliver on work-based learning courses, to professional audiences and in workshop contexts. They can also act as coaches and mentors as part of or an extension of the training delivery. They can be engaged on short-term, long-term or one-off sessions and may be responsible for designing, developing and/or delivering bespoke accredited and unaccredited courses.

Trainers may be highly specialised or expert in their area, with professional competency usually being more important than academic qualifications. However, in order to be effective, even trainers need to know some basic teaching, learning and assessment techniques and strategies, including structured planning and delivery of training. Where trainers are delivering sessions on clients' premises they are expected to abide by both their organisation's policies and procedures and observe those of the host client. Management training and highly technical training may be delivered by trainers who are also freelance consultants, providing expert advice and training as part of a portfolio of professional services. Sometimes trainers specialise in delivering training only.

(c) Tutor

Tutors can take the form of group tutor or personal tutor. Group tutors are likely to occupy more of a pastoral role, providing guidance and support to a group of learners (often a class) and monitoring and reviewing their progress on the course and setting achievement and improvement targets for learners. This will normally take place as part of tutorial sessions, scheduled on a weekly basis outside of lectures and training. Group tutors may outline some course content, but they seldom provide lectures or training during tutorials.

Tutorials, like lectures and training, require some form of scheme of work and lesson plans, but these can be more flexible and adapt to meet the evolving needs of different groups of learners while they are completing their main course. For instance, a group may be experiencing particular difficulties in completing an assignment. The group tutor might liaise with the lecturer and provide dedicated support and guidance in tutorials or as part of additional workshops. Personal tutors occupy a similar role, but liaise and support learners on a more individual basis. They may have a similar subject background to the learner and so can provide more subject specific assistance, whereas group tutors could have a different subject background to their group and so are likely to be less able to provide subject specific assistance.

(d) Assessor

An assessor can also be a lecturer or trainer. However, a lecturer or trainer might not be an assessor. An assessor is someone who formally assesses or marks / grades a learner's work. They are likely to design or share the design of assignment briefs / assessment instruments. They might possess assessor qualifications (these include: A1, A2, D32, D33, Level 3 Award in Understanding the Principles and Practices of Assessment, Level 3 Award in Assessing

Competence in the Work Environment, Level 3 Award in Assessing Vocationally Related Achievement, Level 3 Certificate in Assessing Vocational Achievement).

They would normally be expected to design or contribute towards the design of assignment briefs based on unit assessment criteria and assess work in line with unit assessment criteria. Each course includes modules or units. Each unit contains learning outcomes (these are a 'headline' of what a learner should be able to demonstrate in the evidence they produce as observed or written work). Each learning outcome will include assessment criteria, which are more specific about what the learner must demonstrate.

For example, the first learning outcome for the unit *Understanding Roles, Responsibilities and Relationships in Education and Training* could be to *Understand the teaching role and responsibilities in education and training.* One of the assessment criteria under this learning outcome may be that learners must be able to *Explain the teaching role and responsibilities in education and training.* Assessors would be expected to ensure that assignment briefs or tasks are correctly aligned to the assessment criteria, especially the command verb (in this case 'explain') and that completed work has generated the evidence expected from this assessment criteria.

An assessor would use awarding organisation qualification specifications and unit guides to ensure they are assessing accurately to the assessment criteria. Once assessments have taken place, assessors would usually be expected to standardise their assessments with colleagues. In other words, hold standardisation meetings to make sure that each other is assessing at the right level and accurately and that they agree with the grades they are awarding. They may complete a standardisation form to record the outcomes of the meeting and the grades that have been agreed. Assessors then internally verify another assessor's work, providing that assessor with feedback on the quality of their assessment and feedback to the learner. In some cases, the assessor would need to hold internal verifier qualifications in order to internally verify assessed work. This will depend on the requirements of the awarding organisation concerned.

2. Key aspects of legislation and regulatory requirements relevant to the teaching role

Lecturers, trainers, tutors and assessors will be expected to understand, outline and apply legislative and regulatory requirements and organisational codes of practice that are relevant to their role. There may be some requirements that are purely their responsibility, some that they share with others and some that are entirely the responsibility of others. For example, in relation to health and safety, it is the lecturer's responsibility to make sure that the walkways in the classroom remain unobstructed by chairs or other items during their session, whereas if a chair is broken, the responsibility is shared between the lecturer and their line manager/premises manager to make sure the chair is no longer being used and it is reported to management accordingly, who would be expected to get it repaired or replaced. There are some responsibilities that rest with management alone, such as providing operational computers, lighting, heating and safe fixtures and fittings.

(a) Key *legislation*

Health and Safety at Work etc. Act 1974

Main purpose: to create a safe working environment for everyone. A copy of the Act can be found at: http://www.legislation.gov.uk/ukpga/1974/37

Essential reading:

Health and safety made simple—The basics for your business (HSE)

First aid at work-Your questions answered (HSE)

Workplace requirements and expectations:

1. Health and Safety policy, procedure and statement.
2. Risk assessments:
      (a) Fire risk assessment

(b) Work station assessment

(c) Office risk assessment

(d) Classroom checklist

(e) Risk assessments for work placements and visits.

3. Control of Substances Hazardous to Health (COSHH) (if relevant)

4. Reporting of accidents and near misses:

(a) the Reporting of injuries, Diseases and Dangerous
Occurrences Regulations 1995 (RIDDOR)

(b) accident log book.

5. First Aid policy and procedure.

6. First aid training and first aid kit.

7. Appropriate Health and Safety, First Aid, Fire Safety signage on the premises.

8. Preventative measures:

(a) Monthly fire drills and recording of fire drills carried out

(b) Health and Safety, First Aid, Fire Safety induction
provided to staff and, at a more basic level, to learners.

9. Relevant insurances: e.g. Employers Liability Insurance, Public Liability Insurance.

Who is interested in Health and Safety?:

1. The Health and Safety Executive (HSE), who can fine and prosecute for breaches of Health and Safety.

2. Accreditation bodies: e.g. BAC, ASIC, British Council.

3. Inspection bodies: Ofsted, ISI.

4. Review bodies: QAA.

5. Awarding organisations: e.g. AQA, OCR, Edexcel, City & Guilds.

6. Other stakeholders, e.g. parents and carers of learners, employers of learners.

Data Protection Act 1998

Main purpose: to regulate the processing of and access to personal data.

A copy of the Act can be found at:
http://www.legislation.gov.uk/ukpga/1998/29/contents

Data protection principles (in brief):

1. Personal data shall be processed fairly and lawfully.
2. Personal data shall be obtained only for one or more specified and lawful purposes.
3. Personal data shall be adequate, relevant and not excessive in relation to the purpose or purposes for which they are processed.
4. Personal data shall be accurate and, where necessary, kept up to date.
5. Personal data processed for any purpose shall not be kept for longer than is necessary for that purpose.
6. Personal data shall be processed in accordance with the rights of data subjects under this Act.
7. Appropriate technical and organisational measures shall be taken against unauthorised or unlawful processing of personal data and against accidental loss or destruction of, or damage to, personal data.
8. Personal data shall not be transferred to a country or territory outside the European Economic Area unless that country or territory has an adequate level of protection for the rights and freedoms of data subjects in relation to the processing of personal data.

See further:
http://www.ico.org.uk/for_organisations/data_protection/~/media/documents/library/Data_Protection/Practical_application/the_guide_to_data_protection.pdf

https://www.youtube.com/user/etclondon1/

Requirements and expectations:

1. Organisations processing personal data and their employees or those it engages will comply with the Data Protection Act 1998 and the data protection principles.
2. Organisations processing personal data must register with the Information Commissioner's Office (ICO)
3. ICO can fine organisations that breach data protection requirements.

See further: ICO You Tube channel

Copyright Design and Patents Act 1988

Main purpose: It gives the creators of literary, dramatic, musical and artistic works the right to control the ways in which their material may be used.

A copy of the Act can be found at:
http://www.legislation.gov.uk/ukpga/1988/48/contents

For further information see:
http://www.copyrightservice.co.uk/ukcs/docs/edupack.pdf

See also: Copyright Licensing Agency

Protection of Children Act 1999 & Safeguarding Vulnerable Groups Act 2006

Main purpose of the Acts: to identify persons considered to be unsuitable to work with children or vulnerable adults. Teachers or others who work regularly with children or vulnerable adults are required to undergo an enhanced DBS (Disclosure and Barring Service) check. (These were formerly known as CRB checks.)

A copy of the Acts can be found at:

http://www.legislation.gov.uk/ukpga/1999/14/contents
http://www.legislation.gov.uk/ukpga/2006/47/contents

For further information see: Disclosure and Barring Service (DBS) website and information leaflet.

Children Act 2004

Main purpose of the Act: to make sure safeguarding of children is a paramount consideration. The Act gives effect to the Government's Green Paper *Every Child Matters* and *Every Child Matters: Next Steps.* These focus on 5 outcomes for children:

1. Be healthy
2. Stay safe
3. Enjoy and achieve
4. Make a positive contribution
5. Achieve economic well-being

The Act can be found at:
http://www.legislation.gov.uk/ukpga/2004/31/contents

Education and Skills Act 2008

Main purpose of the Act: this raises the minimum age to 18 for a person wishing to leave education or training (even when employed, individuals under 18 should undergo training or education). This is phased in. In 2013 the leaving age was raised to 17. From 2015, the leaving age was raised to 18.

The Act can be found at:
http://www.legislation.gov.uk/ukpga/2008/25/contents

Apprenticeships, Skills, Children and Learning Act 2009

Main purposes of the Act:
1. It provides a statutory framework for apprenticeships. It creates a right to an apprenticeship for suitably qualified 16-18 year olds.
2. It introduces a right for employees to request time away from their duties to undertake training and places a corresponding duty on employers to consider such requests seriously.
3. It dissolved the Learning and Skills Council and transferred the responsibility for funding education and training for 16-18 year-olds to local authorities.
4. It has led to the creation of the Education and Funding Agency (EFA), the Skills and Funding Agency (SFA), a new regulatory body for qualifications (Ofqual).

The Act can be found at:
http://www.legislation.gov.uk/ukpga/2009/22/contents

Equality Act 2010

This is considered in section 3.

Education Act 2011

Main purposes of the Act: to provide some degree of deregulation and freedom for Further Education (FE) colleges and sixth form colleges.

The Act can be found at:
http://www.legislation.gov.uk/ukpga/2011/21/contents/enacted

(b) Regulatory requirements

Awarding organisations and accreditation, inspection and review bodies all have some minimum requirements and expectations of the learning providers they are associated with. These usually include checking that learning providers have fully implemented policies and procedures in dealing with health and safety, data protection, child protection, safeguarding, equality and diversity, assessment, quality assurance, teaching and learning, assessment malpractice and maladministration, academic appeals, complaints, admissions, staff recruitment and selection, conflict of interest, staff development, refunds and reasonable adjustments and special consideration.

In addition, awarding organisations expect their centres / learning providers to abide by their requirements. This can include periodic visits to check the effectiveness of their resources, teaching, learning, assessment and quality assurance processes. Where internal assessments take place, associated processes are of particular interest. These include assignment briefs, internal verification (i.e. checking the fitness for purpose, reliability, validity and timeliness of assignment briefs and assessments), standardisation (i.e. assessors comparing and agreeing assessments, marks or grades to ensure consistency and reliability of assessments) and authenticity of learner work (i.e. checking that any assessment malpractice, such as plagiarism or cheating, has been sufficiently addressed and measures taken to minimise it and that it is the learner's own work, with learners signing authenticity statements).

Accreditation, inspection and review bodies such as BAC, Ofsted, ISI and QAA all have their own frameworks which they expect the learning providers they accredit, inspect or review to work towards and adhere to. Annual or periodic visits can take place to check that learning providers are continuing to meet the framework requirements.

3. Promoting equality and valuing diversity

Legal requirements outline the promotion of equality and diversity, while awarding organisations and inspection and review bodies expect these to be promoted directly or indirectly. An examination of BAC, ISI and Ofsted inspection frameworks will find direct or indirect reference to equality and diversity.

(a) Equality Act 2010 and Ofsted

The Equality Act 2010 introduced nine protected characteristics. These provide protection against discrimination and, to a limited extent, create opportunities to positively discriminate across two of the protected characteristics (namely 'disability' and 'pregnancy and maternity'). The protected characteristics are as follows:

- Age
- Disability
- Gender reassignment
- Marriage and civil partnership
- Pregnancy and maternity
- Race
- Religion or belief
- Sex
- Sexual orientation

The Act makes it unlawful for further and higher education institutions to discriminate against an applicant or student in relation to:

- admissions

- the provision of education
- access to benefits, facilities or services
- exclusions

It also makes it unlawful to harass or victimise an applicant or student or, in limited circumstances, to discriminate, harass or victimise a former student or to aid another in discriminating, harassing or victimising a student.

Publicly funded organisations are under a legal obligation to promote equality and diversity. This duty goes beyond preventing discrimination. Where learning providers are inspected by Ofsted, equality and diversity is defined in a much broader sense than the Equality Act 2010 and providers are expected to identify and narrow any achievement gaps across different groups of learners, ensure that teaching, learning and assessment promote equality, support diversity and tackle discrimination, victimisation, harassment, stereotyping or bullying. Lecturers are also expected to use materials and teaching methods that foster good relations and are sensitive to and promote equality of opportunity, and lecturers are expected to be aware of and plan for individual learner needs in teaching sessions. Groups of learners are very broadly defined in the Ofsted common inspection framework 2012, including:

- disabled learners
- learners with special needs
- boys/men
- girls/women
- groups of learners whose prior attainment may be different from that of other groups
- those who are academically more or less able
- learners for whom English is an additional language
- minority ethnic learners
- Gypsy, Roma and Traveller learners
- learners qualifying for a bursary scheme award
- looked after children
- lesbian, gay and bisexual learners
- transgender learners
- young carers
- learners from low-income backgrounds
- older learners
- learners of different religions and beliefs

- ex-offenders
- women returners
- teenage mothers
- other vulnerable groups.

Further guidance on the Act as it applies to further and higher education institutions can be found in the publication *Equality Act 2010: Technical Guidance on Further and Higher Education.*

A copy of the Act can be found at:
http://www.legislation.gov.uk/ukpga/2010/15/contents

(b) Learning disabilities, difficulties and medical conditions

A learning provider during student recruitment and enrolment should actively enquire about learning disabilities, learning difficulties and physical disabilities or medical conditions that are likely to adversely affect a student's learning. Learning providers are then expected to make reasonable adjustments to accommodate such conditions. For example, a learner with very poor vision might be provided with materials that have extra-large print or are supplied in alternative formats, while learners that are colour blind could receive handouts that use colours that are recognised as suitable for this condition. Meanwhile, learners with dyslexia could undertake more verbal rather than written assessments and receive detailed verbal feedback, with short written feedback, since these are more sensitive to their learning difficulty. Awarding organisations permit learning providers to apply reasonable adjustments to assessments, where students have a learning or physical disability or learning difficulty. This may include providing extra time for controlled assessments or examinations or using alternative methods of assessment.

(c) Reducing other barriers to learning

Ice breakers can be used to good effect during induction, where students introduce themselves, talk about their background and interests and are encouraged to share something about their culture, race and religion or belief or lack of religion or belief. If carried out with sensitivity, this should develop mutual respect and understanding. Ice breakers can be supplemented with an outline of college policies and procedures that seek to prevent discrimination,

18

harassment and bullying and make explicit to learners the sanctions applicable where any of these are proven. Lecturers are also expected to intervene to prevent any form of hostility, stereotyping, bullying or discrimination in sessions and, where necessary, take appropriate disciplinary action.

4. Identifying and meeting individual learner needs

The correct and timely identification of individual learner needs is essential in ensuring their prior learning is considered, appropriate support is put in place, gaps in knowledge are identified and addressed at an early stage and related achievement and performance targets are set. Learners may start programmes with a range of relevant prior learning. This learning can be certificated (i.e. formal qualification certificates awarded) or experiential (experience based). Awarding organisations and awarding bodies (such as universities, which have degree awarding powers) tend to have systems and processes in place to recognise / accredit prior learning. These can include accreditation of prior certificated learning (APCL) or accreditation of prior experiential learning (APEL) or recognition of prior learning (RPL), which takes account of both prior and experiential learning.

This process is not commonly used, but where it is applied, learners can gain partial or full unit exemptions, with the permission of awarding organisations or awarding bodies. Where colleges are delivering validated programmes in conjunction with universities, the completed APCL and APEL forms would be sent to the university partner for their determination. Awarding organisations also have RPL mapping procedures in place, where RPL can be mapped by assessment criteria per unit, with supporting evidence and then submitted by the learning provider to the awarding organisation. If successful, the learner would gain exemption from one or more units or certain assessment criteria from one or more units.

Initial assessments are used to ensure learners are placed on the correct level of programme suitable for them, often taking account of their prior qualifications and experience and current skills set. It also identifies learner support needs. Diagnostic tests, involving tests for numeracy, literacy, ICT and possibly subject specific tests, can identify in more detail learner support needs before their course commences. Early intervention, with support structures, including additional workshops for literacy, numeracy, ICT or subject specific content, where needed, can have a positive impact on learner performance and results on the main course of study. Where learners have English as an additional language or are not familiar with formal education or the subject being studied, workshops in academic English can assist learners on level 3-8 programmes to meet the academic demands of these programmes, including reading and understanding subject material and writing about the subject using the correct protocols. For instance, the style and approach of answering questions and essays in law are distinct from those of management programmes, which are distinct again from engineering. There may be some commonalities, however, such as Harvard System of Referencing, correctly citing sources used and the approach to effective research.

During the programme, learning providers normally use individual learning plans (ILPs) or their equivalent. These monitor and review learner progress on a regular basis (sometimes on a weekly basis for short courses or termly basis for longer courses) and set achievement and performance targets that learners should be meeting.

Detailed guidance on awarding organisation requirements, unit assessment criteria and the skills needed to succeed in examinations and correctly identifying the level of guidance and support needed by learners are important in ensuring learners are realising their full academic potential. Some lecturers might introduce skills-building sessions very early on in programmes, making sure learners are familiar with assessment criteria, how to structure responses to tasks, undertake different assessment methods, such as delivering presentations, drafting reports, participating in role play and professional discussions and completing examinations, with multiple choice questions, short-answer questions, essay style questions, case studies and data analysis. Learners' prior educational experience of coursework, examinations, internal assessments and work-based assessments will affect the extent to which they need guidance and support in developing the appropriate skills to succeed in their assessments.

Ways to maintain a safe and supportive learning environment

1. Maintaining a safe and supportive learning environment

(a) Safe physical environment

Whether a session is being delivered on the premises managed by the learning provider, on a client's premises or delivered off-site, lecturers have a degree of responsibility to plan for and maintain a safe learning environment for their learners. For instance, there are aspects of the physical environment that are under the direct control of lecturers, such as room layout (assuming that tables and chairs are not fixed to the floor or walls), walk ways and the temporary condition of floors (e.g. being clear of any liquid or spillage). There is also a responsibility to intervene where learners are viewing restricted or inappropriate websites or unauthorised videos or other material. Such intervention, depending on the nature of the material being viewed, could include asking them to stop viewing such content, report the matter to a line manager and/or commence disciplinary proceedings.

Where the matter is of a more permanent nature, such as damaged and loose fixtures and fittings, cracks in the ceiling, uneven floor surfaces, lecturers would be expected to report these as soon as possible to their line managers, who would then be responsible for taking or coordinating corrective action. Although learning providers normally have public liability insurance, they are expected not to be reckless or negligent by ignoring or taking too long to respond to health and safety risks.

Where delivery is going to be off-site, such as a visit, learning providers should have a risk assessment process, where the necessary risks are assessed at the planning stage of the visit by lecturers. If the risks are sufficiently low and any parental consent is obtained for the visit for learners under 18 years of age, the trip should go ahead. Where part or all of the delivery is on a client's or employer's premises, as is standard in work-based learning situations, learning providers would undertake some basic health and safety checks, ensuring that the client or employer adheres to the minimum health and safety requirements.

Examples of risk assessments can be found at the Health and Safety Executive website (http://www.hse.gov.uk/).

(b) Supportive learning environment

A good starting point is to establish clear and enforceable ground rules. These can be based on mutual respect and social agreement and learner contracts (this is discussed in section 2 below). Ground rules can outline certain expectations relating to behaviour, conduct and approach and can be set at the beginning of the programme, during each session and at the beginning of particular activities. Some examples are provided below.

(i) Ground rules at the beginning of the programme

Lecturers and programme leaders can formally outline programme and college expectations of learners, including how they are expected to behave with each other and college staff, attendance, punctuality, completing assignments and so on. Ice breakers, related group activities and practice assignments during induction can be used to underpin these ground rules, with lecturers intervening to enforce such rules where learners are not meeting them.

(ii) Ground rules at the beginning of a session or before an activity

Ground rules may need to be made explicit for new learners or where new activities are being introduced. For instance, where a lecturer is delivering their first PowerPoint presentation to the class, they might want to make explicit when and how learners can ask questions and what they are expected to do during the presentation (e.g. making notes). Ground rules might also need to be outlined before a new assessment method is used, such as role play, delivering a presentation and undertaking a professional dialogue. This establishes boundaries and acceptable protocols of behaviour, conduct and approach to the assessment method being applied.

(iii) Negotiating ground rules

In order for learners to take ownership and responsibility for adhering to ground rules, there needs to be some form of consultation, involvement and negotiation. Where learners feel that they have been consulted, involved and ground rules established by mutual agreement and respect, they are more likely to be followed with minimal intervention or enforcement by lecturers.

(c) Structured learning environment

Schemes of work and lesson plans are often used to ensure that sessions are well-planned, structured and follow-on from each other. Learners tend to prefer a reasonable degree of structure to their learning. This can be outlined at the beginning of each programme and unit with the issue of outline schemes of work and assessment plans for each unit, so that learners know the timeframes they are working to, what they will be learning and when assessments, exams, resubmissions and retakes are likely to take place.

In sessions, lecturers are also usually expected to create content links with past and future sessions. For instance, at the beginning of the session recapping briefly what was covered in the previous session and how it relates to what is being covered in this session, and at the end of the session outlining what will be covered in the next session and any prior preparation or reading / homework required before then. Lecturers are expected to outline what will be covered in the session and the session's objectives (i.e. what learners will have learnt or be able to do at the end of the session). Those undertaking inspection and audit normally consider these elements when observing and grading sessions, since they demonstrate aspects of effective planning and structured delivery.

(d) Individual support

Individual learning plans (ILPs) enable lecturers or tutors to monitor learner progress against set / agreed targets. Where learners have comfortably achieved these targets, more challenging targets might be agreed. Where learners have under-performed, additional activities and support may be considered and mutually agreed. This could include attending workshops or additional sessions. This will only be effective if there are monitoring and reporting processes in place to provide feedback on attendance, punctuality and progress being made by learners that have been referred to workshops or additional sessions. The learning provider, if it is a school or academy, is likely to have individual education plans (IEP's) or their equivalent in place (colleges or training providers are unlikely to have them). IEP's are similar to ILP's, except to the extent that they focus on special educational needs for learners with learning disabilities and learning difficulties.

(e) Pair work and group work

Paired and group working provide opportunities for mutual support, particularly where such working is among mixed ability learners. However, in order for these to work effectively, ground rules need to be set, made explicit and understood by learners. Learners also have to be willing to engage in such pair and group work, which can take some practice and persuasion. This approach to support is likely to be more effective than lecturer-to-learner support in the long run, since learners tend to be more receptive to peer support, guidance and feedback. This activity can be underpinned by self-assessment and peer-assessment activities, where learners initially mark / grade their own work (self-assessment) or initially mark / grade another learner's work (peer-assessment). Learners can then compare their self-assessment and peer assessment with subsequent lecturer marking / grading. Learners are more likely to engage with and internalise assessment / marking criteria where they undertake self-assessment and peer-assessment and develop some of the skills needed for independent learning.

2. Promoting appropriate behaviour and respect for others

(a) Policies and procedures

Most learning providers are expected to have a range of policies and procedures in place to manage learner behaviour and respect for others. Such policies are usually required by various stakeholders, including management, awarding organisations and inspection and review bodies. Policies and procedures in this area include those relating to equality and diversity, bullying and harassment. They are linked to disciplinary procedures where learners have transgressed such policies and procedures.

However, their effectiveness depends in large part on learners being made aware of their existence and consequences, being able to understand what they mean (i.e. what amounts to harassment, bullying, discrimination and stereotyping) and being reminded of them periodically or where an issue is emerging relating to these. For instance, where learners have said something discriminatory in class, lecturers should intervene and correct such conduct and make learners aware of their responsibilities and the learning provider's expectations of them. Immediate intervention and rapid follow-up to emerging and actual incidents, even if trivial, would underpin a zero-tolerance approach. Where zero-tolerance is used tactfully, fairly and in a proportionate manner in relation to behaviour related issues, it should lead to better learner behaviour and fewer transgressions.

(b) Learner contracts

Learner contracts or learner agreements are signed by learners at the beginning of the programme. Detailed learner contracts outline what the learner can expect from the learning provider and their rights and actions they can take if the learning provider falls short of their duties / quality of service. Similarly, learner contracts also outline what the learning provider expects of the learner and the consequences of the learner breaching the student contract or the learning provider's policies and procedures. These tend to set the ground rules and make expectations of both parties explicit. Simple learner contracts just outline what is expected of the learner while on their programme. However, in practice, the effectiveness of student contracts in encouraging good behaviour or conduct is limited, except where they are actively enforced. Where sessions are engaging, the learning environment inviting and inclusive and learning materials aligned to the interests of learners, behaviour is likely to be better.

(c) Inclusive learning environment and learning resources

The characteristics of an inclusive learning environment include producing accessible handouts (i.e. using an appropriate print size and font type, using colours that are sensitive to learners who experience colour-blindness), understanding and responding effectively to individual learning and support needs, using engaging assessment methods and providing workshops on different assessment methods where learners lack the skills to be successful in these assessment methods (e.g. presentations, role play, report writing and professional discussions) and taking account of different learning styles (i.e. Visual, Auditory, Read and write, Kinaesthetic – VARK).

Case studies can also be matched to learner interests. For instance, those under the age of 40 are more likely to be interested in mobile technology, while those under the age of 30 are more likely to actively engage with social media, such as Twitter, Facebook and You Tube. Case studies that take account of learner interests should increase learner engagement and encourage achievement. This should also have a positive impact on their behaviour and attitude in sessions, especially where sessions are delivered in an engaging and fun way (one example of this could include increasing learner participation in sessions and creating opportunities to share ideas and experiences).

The relationships between teachers and other professionals in education and training

1. Working with other professionals

The extent to which lecturers work with other professionals depends on the learning provider's size, structure, culture, available resources, nature of provision and type of learner.

(a) Planning

Lecturers tend to meet with colleagues, line managers and programme leaders to plan course content, assessment schedules and delivery timescales. The greater the number of lecturers delivering on the course, the greater the need for detailed and co-ordinated planning and monitoring, including regular meetings to review and evaluate the extent to which delivery is going according to plan.

(b) Sharing assessment outcomes / learner progress

In order to ensure learners remain on target and progress internally and externally to other courses and in order to ensure that assessment outcomes are in line with learning provider expectations, lecturers are expected to periodically report on predicted assessment outcomes / grades, actual outcomes / grades and resubmission opportunities. With a few awarding organisations limiting the resubmission and retake opportunities for some of their qualifications and moves elsewhere to fewer retake opportunities during a programme, the sharing of assessment outcomes becomes crucial to ensuring learner achievement is maximised. Reporting on assessment outcomes may also highlight underlying learner needs.

(c) Communicating learner needs

Effective and timely learner unit and task tracking systems, initial assessments and diagnostics, additional workshops and tutorial sessions should provide most of the information needed to identify learner needs. These can then be discussed at regular team and leadership meetings to co-ordinate department and college level strategies to address learner needs and identify support strategies. Support strategies, however, have implications for staffing, resourcing, funding and timetabling, as well as learner perceptions. Therefore, support needs have to be negotiated, their impact considered and a strategy agreed with a range of stakeholders in order to create 'buy-in' or commitment (learners often have a negative perception of additional learning workshops or support strategies).

(d) Negotiating support for learners

Learners may need a range of support. This can include additional workshops, additional learning support (in the form of literacy, numeracy, ICT, subject specific and support related to learning disabilities and learning difficulties) and reasonable adjustments applied to assessments and examinations. Additional workshops need to be staffed and timetabled, their impact monitored and learners encouraged to attend. Therefore, lecturers would need to discuss these with their line manager, who in turn may discuss them with their superiors and budget holders for learning support. Once agreed, learners would need to be approached and encouraged or required to attend (depending on learning provider policies, procedures and approach to learning support).

Where reasonable adjustments need to be made to assessment methods, assessment timing or extra time or additional resources (such as a scribe or word processor) for exams, there is likely to be some discussion with the awarding organisation concerned. Awarding organisations do provide some discretion to their centres / learning providers to allocate some adjustments or extra time for assessments, and this varies among awarding organisations. Reasonable adjustments and support can also have implications for internal quality assurance (i.e. any reasonable adjustment or extra time provided must be proportionate and must not compromise the validity or reliability of the assessment or provide the learner concerned with an unfair advantage).

(e) Contributing to internal quality assurance

Where a learning provider is responsible for internally assessing its learners through observing practicals, presentations, role plays, professional discussions and for marking assignments and reports, these have to be quality assured. Quality assurance starts at the assignment brief design stage. A lecturer or assessor would normally draft an assignment brief or make some amendments to one already provided by an awarding organisation. These would then need to be formally checked by a colleague to ensure they are fit for purpose. If not, changes would need to be made before being issued to learners. Once learners have completed their assignments and marking commences, lecturers are likely to meet for pre-assessment standardisation, where they compare each other's marking of learner work to agree whether it has been assessed at the right level, the assessment is accurate and reliable and whether they agree with the mark or grade given. If they are in agreement, marking continues with the remainder of the work and a further standardisation meeting may be held to confirm consistency of marking / grading.

A sample would then be internally verified, which allows a colleague to provide feedback on the assessment undertaken by another lecturer. This cycle of internal quality assurance is then checked by the awarding organisation through a postal sample of internally verified learner work across one or two units of a programme, or more widely or through centre visits. External verifiers / external examiners normally undertake visits to centres to check that internal quality assurance processes and assessments are in line with awarding organisation expectations. Reports are then issued, which may have essential actions or recommendations that need to be followed-up within a specified timeframe. An example of the internal quality assurance process can be found in the *BTEC Centre Guide to Managing Quality*, published by Pearson.

Learning providers may use peer reviews or peer observations to share good practice and quality assure teaching sessions. Peer reviews or observations include lecturers observing colleagues' sessions and providing feedback to each other. This may be used as a performance management and/or developmental tool linked to support or training. In any case, the principal aim is to maintain, improve or enhance quality of teaching and learning in sessions. Lecturers might be included in board and committee meetings to discuss new or amended policies and procedures that affect them. Their feedback on the draft policies and procedures could lead to their refinement before being implemented.

(f) Liaising with referral agencies

Further education colleges tend to have detailed systems and processes in place to refer learners that are at risk of harm or with mental health issues or presenting safeguarding issues internally first to a designated person and then on to a relevant external agency. This may include the completion of a multi-agency referral form by a designated person, with input from lecturers. Some learners may have a social services and mental health team supporting them and their complex needs. Lecturers might need to liaise with the designated person in the college and with the external team to provide an update of any issues or further support needs or progress being made. The learner's support teams may inform the designated person and lecturer of the learner's condition so far as it impacts on their attendance and learning (e.g. the learner is not able to manage strict assessment deadlines, since pressure exacerbates their mental condition. This condition is likely to justify extending assignment submission deadlines).

2. The boundaries between the teaching role and other professional roles

(a) Personal boundaries

As with most roles, the lecturing role has its limitations. Personal limitations include skills and experience. For instance, newly qualified lecturers may lack the skills and experience to competently draft an assignment brief or undertake robust quality assurance or prepare learners effectively for their examinations. In such instances, the lecturer may need support and training and should liaise with more experienced lecturers familiar with these areas. Lecturers might not have the requisite qualifications, skills or experience to deal with complex medical, emotional or mental health needs of learners and would therefore need to refer the matter on to their line manager or an appropriately qualified and experienced individual in the organisation. Job descriptions and person specifications should also assist the lecturer in identifying the extent of their duties and responsibilities and therefore the boundaries of their role.

(b) Professional boundaries

Job descriptions provide a good starting point to identify professional boundaries. Department and organisational structures and line management roles create an outline of respective duties and responsibilities. For instance, even where a lecturer possesses more experience and expertise than a colleague, they may have less formal authority to deal with particular duties, such as quality assurance, since the learning provider has allocated those duties to their colleague. In this situation, although the lecturer's personal skills and aptitude are greater than the colleague's, professional boundaries must still be respected, with the colleague's authority to deal with quality assurance matters being accepted.

Departments usually have line management and communication protocols, including those relating to chairing of meetings, committees and boards. Lecturers may be allocated additional responsibility within these protocols and line management structures. As such, they need to ensure that they are acting within their job description and not exceeding their authority. Some matters might need to be escalated to a line manager, while others may need to be referred to another professional in the organisation. Understanding these boundaries assists in maintaining effective management, communication and accountability. Policies and procedures should outline the correct person to contact and correct protocol to follow.

3. Points of referral to meet individual learner needs

(a) Organisation systems and procedures

All learning providers will have systems and procedures in place, although the resources committed to these will vary depending on size, complexity of provision and finance available. In most further education colleges there will be teams dealing with administration, additional learning support, student services, virtual learning environment, website and premises. Lecturers would be expected to know who to refer particular enquiries or issues to in the organisation. For example, issues or enquiries about enrolment, course registrations and examination entries will normally be referred to registration and examinations teams. Where the application form and outcomes of initial assessment and diagnostic assessment indicate learning support needs, the referral would be to a relevant line manager and the additional learning support team.

Where technical changes have to be made to the virtual learning environment (e.g. new sections added) or changes made to the website, the IT team will need to be contacted and possibly also the marketing and teaching and learning teams. Where there are health and safety related enquiries or concerns, these would be referred to the premises team. Policies and procedures related to the above areas will usually outline the referrals process, with details of who to contact initially and in case of an urgent matter.

(b) External agencies

Policies and procedures should also outline the protocols for referring matters internally and, where required, externally. Where a learner has a severe learning or physical disability or major learning difficulty, a lecturer would need to refer the matter to the examinations team, who in turn would contact the awarding organisations concerned to obtain permission to apply reasonable adjustments, such as allocating a scribe, providing a word processor in an examination and requesting 50% or 100% extra time for an examination. In case of assessment malpractice, a lecturer would be expected to report the matter to a line manager and the exams team; this would trigger an internal investigation. A member of the senior management team would then need to consider reporting the incident to the awarding organisation concerned. Failure to do so could result in sanctions being applied to the learning provider by the awarding organisation concerned.

Learning providers might also have whistleblowing procedures, where a lecturer or other employee can disclose a major concern to an external agency regarding a range of matters, including those affecting learners, and such disclosure, if valid and justified, should provide them with a degree of protection from subsequent disciplinary proceedings, victimisation and dismissal. Where a learner makes a disclosure to a lecturer, the lecturer would need to contact a designated person at the learning provider responsible for safeguarding, who would then report the matter externally to a relevant agency, where needed.

Command verbs (used in this unit)

COMMAND VERB	DEFINITION
Describe	Provide an extended range of detailed factual information about the topic or item in a logical way.
Explain	Make something clear to someone by describing or revealing relevant information in more detail.
Summarise	Give the main ideas or facts in a concise way.

Glossary of key terms used in this textbook

TERM	DEFINITION
Accreditation of prior learning (APL)	APL is the generic term for the accreditation of prior learning, whether the result of a formal course or learning through experience. (APL is the term normally used by awarding bodies, such as universities. The equivalent used by awarding organisations is RPL.)
Accreditation of prior certificated learning (APCL)	APCL is based on certified (or certificated) learning following a formal course of study at another learning provider or institute. (APCL is the term normally used by awarding bodies, such as universities.)
Accreditation of prior experiential learning (APEL)	APEL is based on experiential learning - learning achieved through experience, rather than on a formal course of study. (APEL is the term normally used by awarding bodies, such as universities.)
Assessment criteria	Each learning outcome contains assessment criteria that are used to assess the learner evidence submitted. These are normally related to grades.
Assessor	This refers to the person responsible for making decisions about whether learners' work achieves the national standard required for certification (e.g. whether assessment criteria and any related grade descriptors have been met).
Awarding body	Although the terms awarding body and awarding organisation have been used to mean the same thing, an awarding body is normally an organisation with degree awarding powers, such as a university.
Awarding organisation	Although the terms awarding organisation and awarding body have been used to mean the same thing, awarding organisations are normally regulated by Ofqual and do not possess degree awarding powers.
Command verb	This is a verb that requires a specific action and is normally placed at the beginning of an assessment criteria, such as 'outline', 'describe', 'explain', 'analyse', 'evaluate'.
Diagnostic assessment	This is an assessment used to discover a candidate's strengths and weaknesses. It is often used to assess a learner's literacy, numeracy, ICT or subject specific skills or knowledge.
Diversity	There is no fixed or legal definition for diversity. It can be viewed as recognising and celebrating difference.

Equality	"Equality is about ensuring that every individual has an equal opportunity to make the most of their lives and talents, and believing that no one should have poorer life chances because of where, what or whom they were born, what they believe, or whether they have a disability." http://www.equalityhumanrights.com/private-and-public-sector-guidance/education-providers/secondary-education-resources/useful-information/understanding-equality
External Examiner (EE)	An external examiner is a person from another awarding body or awarding organisation, who monitors the assessment, moderation, double marking, standardisation and internal verification process of a learning provider for fairness, academic standards and quality assurance.
External moderation	An external moderator ensures that a learning provider is continuing to meet an awarding organisation's academic and quality standards by reassessing candidate's work. This normally applies to coursework.
External Verifier (EV)	An external verifier is appointed by an awarding organisation to ensure that the learning provider's / centre's own quality assurance systems are being implemented effectively in order to maintain national standards by • providing information, advice and support to centres • certifying delivery/assessment practice and centre procedures (e.g. ensuring that assessment decisions are consistent with national standards) • maintaining records of visits and providing feedback (including essential actions, recommendations and areas of good practice)
Inclusive learning	This is about ensuring that all learners have sufficient opportunity to be included and actively involved in the learning process and that they are treated fairly, equally and their differences are recognised, accommodated and where relevant celebrated.
Initial assessment	Initial assessment is a formal and informal process that identifies each learner's starting point. It helps to identify learners' current levels of ability and their

	need for support and is often used to place learners at a particular level of study.
Internal verification	This is a centre devised quality assurance process which assures the assessment against the awarding organisation unit grading criteria (i.e. making sure that learners' responses meet the requirements of the unit assessment criteria) and that assignment briefs are fit for purpose (i.e. are capable of allowing learners to generate the evidence required to pass the unit).
Internal Verifier	This is a member of staff able to verify assessor decisions, and validate assignments. The Internal Verifier records findings, gives assessor feedback, and oversees remedial action
Learner contract	A basic learner contract will outline the expected conduct from a learner, such as attendance, punctuality, abiding by the organisations policies and procedures, etc.
Learning aims/outcomes	This is what the learner should know, understand or be able to do as a result of completing the unit.
Lesson plans	A lesson plan is a lecturer's guide to delivering a particular session, including session aims, objectives, assessment strategies, session content and timeframe, learning resources to be used and lecturer and learner activities.
Mapping of recognition of prior learning	This is a formal process often devised by the awarding organisation where the learning provider maps the learner's prior learning (certificated and/or experiential) against each learning aim/outcome and assessment criteria of a unit and then submits it to the awarding organisation for consideration. If successful, the learner does not have to complete those assessment criteria that have been recognised as having been achieved through prior learning.
Ofqual	The Office of Qualifications and Examinations Regulation (Ofqual) regulates qualifications, examinations and assessments in England and vocational qualifications in Northern Ireland. Ofqual is a non-ministerial department.
Peer assessment	Peer assessment involves learners taking responsibility for assessing the work of their peers against set assessment criteria.
Pre-assessment standardisation	Internal pre-assessment standardisation is a process within a centre / learning provider for checking an

	initial sample of internal assessments / marking / grading to ensure it is consistent across all assessors before assessors continue assessing / marking / grading. This process only applies to internally assessed learner work.
Qualification specification	awarding organisations publish qualification specifications for their centres / learning providers to use in developing and delivering the awarding organisation courses. The qualification specification sets out what is required of the learner in order to achieve the qualification, it contains information about permitted unit combinations and information specific to managing and delivering the qualification(s) including specific quality assurance requirements.
Reasonable adjustment	In the context of learning providers, a reasonable adjustment is an alteration that a learning provider makes to enable a disabled learner to continue to carry out their duties without being at a disadvantage compared to other learners.
Recognition of prior learning (RPL)	RPL recognises prior learning, whether the result of a formal course of study or learning through experience. RPL is the term used by awarding organisations and is equivalent to APL.
Safeguarding	Safeguarding is a term which is broader than 'child protection' and relates to the action taken to promote the welfare of children and protect them from harm. Safeguarding is defined in Working together to safeguard children 2013 as: <ul><li>protecting children from maltreatment</li><li>preventing impairment of children's health and development</li><li>ensuring that children grow up in circumstances consistent with the provision of safe and effective care and</li><li>taking action to enable all children to have the best outcomes</li></ul>
Schemes of work	A scheme of work is a guideline that defines the structure and content of a course. It maps out clearly how resources (e.g. books, equipment, time) and class activities (e.g. lecturing, group work, practicals, discussions) and assessment strategies (e.g. tests, assignments, homework) will be used to ensure that the learning outcomes and assessment criteria or

	assessment objectives of the course are met successfully. It will normally include times and dates. The scheme of work is usually an interpretation of a qualification specification and unit or module guides.
Self-assessment	Self-assessment requires learners to reflect on their own work and judge how well they have performed in relation to the assessment criteria.
Standardisation	Internal standardisation is a process within a centre / learning provider for checking that internal assessment / marking / grading is accurate and consistent across all assessors. This process only applies to internally assessed learner work.
Standards Verifier (SV)	This is an external verification process used to check centre assignments and assessment against national standards, and internal verification processes.
Unit guide	These outline the unit aims, learning outcomes, assessment criteria, unit content, grading criteria and provide some guidance.

STRUCTURING EFFECTIVE RESPONSES TO MEET THE REQUIREMENTS OF THE UNIT

Understanding the bigger picture

Awarding organisations offer the Certificate in Education and Training qualification. Learning providers seek centre recognition / approval and qualification approval to run this and other qualifications. The qualification is internally assessed by the learning provider using a range of assessment methods and externally monitored by an awarding organisation to ensure that its centres (i.e. learning providers) are meeting its quality assurance requirements for managing and delivering the qualification. The awarding organisations are in turn regulated by Ofqual, which seeks to monitor their compliance with the *General Conditions of Recognition*[1], as well as related conditions.

You might well be thinking "why and how is this relevant to me passing the qualification?". Well, it means that learning providers are limited in how they internally assess the qualification. Although they have a degree of discretion in selecting assessment methods, these must be appropriate and fit for purpose, in that they must generate the evidence required by the qualification. External monitoring normally takes the form of an external verifier, who is contracted or employed by the awarding organisation and possesses sufficient subject expertise, to monitor centre compliance with awarding organisation requirements. Where there are issues of compliance, the awarding organisation could delay the issuing of qualification certificates until the issues are rectified. Centres that have good practices in place and have been operating over a certain period of time might have 'direct claims status', which means that they have fewer external verifier visits. The upshot of all this that a learning provider must not deviate from the learning outcomes and assessment criteria in the qualification. Deviation can include the following:

- *Over-assessing*: requiring more evidence than is actually required, including elements that are not needed to meet the assessment criteria;
- *Under-assessing*: requiring less evidence than is actually required;
- *Misalignment with command verbs*: each assessment criteria has a command verb, such as 'summarise', 'describe', 'explain'. Each of these has a different meaning and therefore affect the quantity and quality of evidence generated. Where the task uses a command verb,

---

[1]https://www.gov.uk/government/uploads/system/uploads/attachment_data/file/371266/2014-11-03-general-conditions-of-recognition-november.pdf (last accessed on 16/05/2015)

such as 'evaluate' instead of 'summarise', it will be clearly over-assessing the candidate, whereas if it used the command verb 'summarise' instead of 'explain' there is a high likelihood that it will be under-assessing the candidate.

The implications of this are that while learning providers can write their own assignments, assessments, worksheets, tasks and select from a broad range of assessment methods, they must not deviate from the learning outcomes and assessment criteria in the qualification. Each awarding organisation makes available a copy of its qualification specification or similar document that contain the qualification structure, learning outcomes and assessment criteria and, in many cases, guidance and suggestions on delivery and assessment strategies. Therefore, the information provided in this textbook will remain relevant regardless of the variations in the assessment instruments used and assessment methods applied.

In the event of a conflict between the suggested response structure in this textbook and your learning provider's expectations, please follow their requirements. After all, there can be some variations in the structure and content of the response given or emphasis added.

We will unpack the requirements of the learning outcomes and assessment criteria for this unit. Learning outcomes are things the learner should know, understand or be able to do as a result of completing the unit, while each learning outcome has assessment criteria that are used to assess the learner evidence submitted. In order to successfully complete a unit, all assessment criteria must be successfully achieved. The units, learning outcomes and assessment criteria are identical across the awarding organisations certificating the Certificate in Education and Training, although the guidance and suggested delivery and assessment methods to be used are likely to vary.

Each assessment criteria includes a command verb. The command verbs used in this unit are as follows (together with a suggested definition).

COMMAND VERB	DEFINITION
Describe	Provide an extended range of detailed factual information about the topic or item in a logical way.
Explain	Make something clear to someone by describing or revealing relevant information in more detail.
Summarise	Give the main ideas or facts in a concise way.

Understanding Roles, Responsibilities and Relationships in Education and Training

This unit's learning outcomes and assessment criteria are as follows:

Learning outcomes		Assessment criteria	
1.	Understand the teaching role and responsibilities in education and training	1.1	*Explain* the teaching role and responsibilities in education and training
		1.2	*Summarise* key aspects of legislation, regulatory requirements and codes of practice relating to own role and responsibilities
		1.3	*Explain* ways to promote equality and value diversity
		1.4	*Explain* why it is important to identify and meet individual learner needs
2.	Understand ways to maintain a safe and supportive learning environment	2.1	*Explain* ways to maintain a safe and supportive learning environment
		2.2	*Explain* why it is important to promote appropriate behaviour and respect for others
3.	Understand the relationships between teachers and other professionals in education and training	3.1	*Explain* how the teaching role involves working with other professionals
		3.2	*Explain* the boundaries between the teaching role and other professional roles
		3.3	*Describe* points of referral to meet the individual needs of learners

Learning outcome		Assessment criteria	
1.	Understand the teaching role and responsibilities in education and training	1.1	*Explain* the teaching role and responsibilities in education and training

Explain the teaching role in education and training

- Select two or more roles from: lecturer, trainer, assessor, instructor
- Describe what those roles involve, in particular focusing on teaching, learning and assessment,
- Give some supporting examples of teaching, learning and assessment (e.g. "a lecturer plans and delivers sessions to learners, using a range of learning resources, such as ..... A lecturer may also be responsible for checking learning through the use of questions and answers ..... may set and mark internal assignments .... "). If possible, make the example specific to a particular subject and qualification (e.g. "In A level Chemistry, the lecturer guides learners on setting-up experiments and monitors and assesses their performance based on the experiments ...").

Explain the responsibilities in education and training

- Outline the range of responsibilities, including reference to some or all of the following:
    - Enforcement of the learning provider's policies and procedures related to any aspect of teaching, learning, assessment, health and safety and equality and diversity;
    - Course and lesson planning, such as schemes of work, lesson plans and learning materials;
    - Administering and recording assessments;
    - Working with others – this can be cross-referenced with assessment criteria 3.1 and 3.2 of this unit (i.e. you could complete that criteria first and then complete this part and cross-reference accordingly (e.g. "this is discussed in more detail, with supporting examples, in tasks .... below.")
- Provide some supporting examples for the above.

Structuring the response

This is probably the hardest part. You have gathered the information, collated it and provided supporting examples, but will another person reading it find it easy to understand or be able to follow it?, is there a logical structure to the response or is it still ambiguous in places? Your responses need to demonstrate that you understand the task or assessment criterion and have provided sufficient information and supporting evidence to answer it.

Possible response structure:

1. List three or more teaching roles;
2. Outline at least three roles;
3. Focus and develop a description of two of those roles;
4. Outline how a session is planned;
5. Outline, with supporting examples what is involved during teaching, learning and assessment;
6. List three or more responsibilities;
7. Describe, with supporting examples, how those responsibilities are carried out.

Your assessment tasks might specify the roles you need to consider and also the range of responsibilities. If so, you will need to adapt the above accordingly.

Assessment criterion 1.2

1.	Understand the teaching role and responsibilities in education and training	1.2	*Summarise* key aspects of legislation, regulatory requirements and codes of practice relating to own role and responsibilities

Summarise key aspects of legislation

- List the range of relevant legislation in order of importance, with the one you will be affected by the most being the first in the list (e.g. health and safety is probably the most important, in part because the consequences of its breach can be serious and life threatening);
- Focus on a small selection of legislation to explore in more detail;
- Suppose that you have selected the Health and Safety at Work etc. Act 1974, the Equality Act 2010 and the Data Protection Act 1998. You then

need to select key elements from each of these. For the Equality Act 2010 it may be to outline the nine protected characteristics and who they protect and how, while for the Health and Safety at Work etc. Act 1974 the range of risk assessments could be outlined and when they apply, and for the Data Protection Act 1998 the data protection principles can be outlined;

- Provide one or more practical supporting examples for each of these legislation, e.g. making reasonable adjustments to assessments (Equality Act 2010), carrying out risk assessments for external learner visits (Health and Safety at Work etc. Act 1974), and using an encrypted USB/Flash drive to hold personal data, such as examination results for learners (Data Protection Act 1998).

Summarise key aspects of regulatory requirements

- List external regulatory bodies that could affect your work directly and/or indirectly through learning providers' policies and procedures, e.g. awarding organisations (they will normally have a direct impact on your work, such as what is delivered, its timeframe and how it is delivered) and inspection or review bodies, such as Ofsted, ISI, BAC, QAA (they will impact the learning provider and management, who will need to ensure that teaching, learning and assessment policies and practices are in line with their expectations);
- Select the most relevant aspects from awarding organisations and inspection and review bodies that affect your role (e.g. assignments have to be in line with awarding organisation qualification specifications and assessment criteria; lessons need to be effectively planned and differentiated to meet all learners' needs and, in turn, to meet the expectations of inspection and review bodies);
- Provide supporting practical examples.

Summarise key aspects of codes of practice relating to own role and responsibilities

- List the internal and external codes of practice that are relevant to your role (i.e. codes of practice and conduct within the learning provider and the *Professional Standards for Teachers and Trainers in Education and Training – England[2]*);

- Outline their scope and purpose (i.e. who do they apply to, how do they apply / what do they expect and what do they seek to achieve?);
- Outline how they affect your role.

Possible response structure:

1. Brief introduction and listing of legislation, regulation and codes of practice relevant to your role;
2. Select and summarise key aspects of:
   (a) three Acts of Parliament (legislation),
   (b) an awarding organisation and an inspection or review body's requirements or expectations that are most relevant to your role,
   (c) one internal and one external code of practice or professional standard;
3. Give one or more detailed supporting examples for each Act, an awarding organisation and/or inspection body and for an internal code of practice and/or an external professional standard.

Assessment criterion 1.3

	Learning outcomes		Assessment criteria
1.	Understand the teaching role and responsibilities in education and training	1.3	*Explain* ways to promote equality and value diversity

Explain ways to promote equality

- Provide a brief definition of equality;
- Describe how individual learning needs can be identified and what support can be provided;

---

[2] http://www.et-foundation.co.uk/wp-content/uploads/2014/05/4991-Prof-standards-A4_4-2.pdf

- Outline the reasonable adjustments that can be made in relation to assessment and feedback relevant to learners with physical disability, learning difficulties and medical conditions and how such adjustments can reduce their barriers to learning (e.g. providing a learner that has dyslexia with additional time to complete an assessment or examination should reduce the disadvantage faced by them due to their learning difficulty, since it normally takes such learners more time to process written text. The additional time should compensate for this.);
- Also consider the notion of 'promotion'. This requires commitment and positive steps to ensure equality is in place in systems and practices;
- Outline strategies to tackle discrimination (e.g. challenging discriminatory comments and behaviour in class, having in place learner contracts and establishing ground rules)

Explain ways to value diversity

- Provide a brief definition of diversity;
- Describe the 'carrot and stick' approach to valuing diversity (i.e. having incentives or a positive / enjoyable approach to valuing diversity, such as cultural celebrations, ice breakers and social events for diverse learners, awareness raising of different faiths and traditions. Having sanctions where learners devalue diversity, normally activated where learners have not adhered to their learner contracts or equality and diversity policies and procedures. In such cases disciplinary procedures could be activated by the learning provider);
- Give supporting examples wherever possible.

Possible response structure:

1. Brief definitions of equality and diversity;
2. Describe how individual learning needs can be identified and promoted, with supporting examples to ensure equality;
3. Describe incentives or positive approaches to valuing diversity and sanctions for devaluing it, together with supporting examples for both.

Learning outcomes		Assessment criteria
Understand the teaching role and responsibilities in education and training	1.4	**Explain** why it is important to identify and meet individual learner needs

Explain why it is important to identify individual learner needs

- Outline the different ways that learner needs can be identified, including by recognition of prior learning, initial assessment, diagnostic assessment and individual learning plans (ILP's);
- Describe what the benefits could be for the learner and learning provider if the individual learner needs are accurately identified in a timely manner and what the issues or drawbacks could be if they are not;
- Give specific examples relating to recognition of prior learning and/or initial assessment and diagnostic assessment.

Explain why it is important to meet individual learner needs

- Outline how individual learner needs could be met (e.g. additional learning support, reasonable adjustments to assessments for learners with disabilities, learning difficulties or medical conditions);
- Describe what the benefits could be for the learner and learning provider of meeting individual learner needs and drawbacks of not meeting them (including possible legal repercussions under the Equality Act 2010);
- Give specific examples of meeting individual learner needs, such as adjusting timetables for those who have been exempted from some course units due to recognition of prior learning and extra time in examinations or additional support in assessment for learners with disabilities and learning difficulties.

Possible response structure:

1. Outline how learner needs can be identified and met;
2. Describe the benefits to the learner and the learning provider of accurately identifying and meeting individual learner needs in a timely manner;
3. Describe the drawbacks to the learner and learning provider of not accurately identifying and meeting individual learner needs in a timely manner;
4. Provide supporting examples of such needs, including reference to disabilities, learning difficulties, medical conditions, ILP's and additional learning support.

Assessment criterion 2.1

Learning outcomes		Assessment criteria	
2.	Understand ways to maintain a safe and supportive learning environment	2.1	*Explain* ways to maintain a safe and supportive learning environment

Explain ways to maintain a safe learning environment

- Outline relevant health and safety legislation and requirements, including risk assessments of the premises, in particular the classroom;
- Describe ways to keep the classroom environment safe, including clear walkways, reporting defective or damaged floors, ceilings, furniture, taking preventative measures to deal with slips and trips;
- Outline risk assessments for external visits;
- Outline how such measures would ensure that a safe learning environment is maintained.

Explain ways to maintain a supportive learning environment

- List possible support mechanisms, including a structured learning environment, individual learning support, additional learning support,

- pair and group working (and how it encourages peer support) and negotiation of ground rules;
- From this list select three main areas you would like to focus on. Then describe how each of those maintains a supportive learning environment;
- Also consider what steps can be taken if one or more support strategies is not proving to be effective; could other support strategies be implemented instead of or in addition to these?
- Provide supporting examples for each of the three support elements or strategies identified.

Possible response structure:

1. Outline health and safety legislation and procedures, such as risk assessments and list support mechanisms available to learning providers;
2. Describe how to keep the classroom environment safe and undertaking risk assessments when taking learners on visits or trips. Make reference to the Health and Safety Executive and their guidelines, where appropriate;
3. Describe at least three support mechanisms or strategies to support learners;
4. Provide supporting examples for the above.

Assessment criterion 2.2

Learning outcomes		Assessment criteria	
2.	Understand ways to maintain a safe and supportive learning environment	2.2	*Explain* why it is important to promote appropriate behaviour and respect for others

Explain why it is important to promote appropriate behaviour

- List the methods or strategies to ensure appropriate behaviour is maintained, including learning provider policies and procedures relating to equality and diversity, bullying, harassment, learner contracts, peer working, inclusion;
- Describe the consequences (e.g. benefits) for the learner, other learners, staff and the learning provider generally of having robust

systems, practices and a culture in place that promotes appropriate behaviour (you might want to consider the impact on effective learning, with minimum disruption in the classroom and the impact on the learners' future behaviour when progressing on to a higher level course or employment);

- Describe the consequences (e.g. drawbacks) for the learner, other learners, staff and the learning provider generally of not having robust systems and practices in place;
- Provide supporting examples, wherever possible, for the above.

Explain why it is important to promote respect for others

- Outline what is meant by 'respect', referring to not discriminating or making rude or prejudicial statements about other people or cultures, not stereotyping, and recognising and accepting that other people may have different views;
- Describe what the likely consequences are for the learner, other learners, staff and the learning provider generally of promoting respect for others and where respect is <u>not</u> promoted for others (you might want to consider the impact on learning, motivation, self-esteem, future conduct in further / higher education or employment and its implications);
- Provide supporting examples, wherever possible, for the above.

Possible response structure:

1. List / outline methods and strategies for maintaining and encouraging appropriate behaviour and what could amount to 'respect for others';
2. Describe the likely consequences for the learner, other learners, staff and the learning provider generally of promoting or failing to promote appropriate behaviour and respect for others, providing supporting examples wherever possible;
3. Acknowledge that behaviour and respect applies to everyone, including the conduct and respect shown by lecturers / trainers / assessors to learners. You might want to explore this aspect with an example to 'round-off' your response.

Learning outcomes		Assessment criteria	
3.	Understand the relationships between teachers and other professionals in education and training	3.1	*Explain* how the teaching role involves working with other professionals

Explain how the teaching role involves working with other professionals

- List the likely opportunities to work with others, including peers when planning and coordinating courses, resources and delivery, quality assuring the units and programme, communicating to peers and line managers about learner support needs, behaviour and progress and liaising with referral agencies;
- Select at least three examples of working with others from the list above and describe what would normally be involved in such working. You might want to consider examining working with professionals internal to the learning provider and those external to it, depending on the information available and your preference;
- Make sure that you limit yourself to the teaching role, although this can extend to quality assurance and pastoral activities depending on the job description.

Possible response structure:

1. Recognise the scope of the teaching role and that it may include some quality assurance, pastoral and management responsibilities;
2. List internal and external opportunities to work with other professionals, providing some supporting examples;
3. Describe three examples of working with others;
4. Identify that your need to and extent of working with others may depend on your personal skills and experience and professional responsibilities (teaching and beyond). This is optional, but would provide a good link to assessment criterion 3.2 below.

Learning outcomes		Assessment criteria	
3.	Understand the relationships between teachers and other professionals in education and training	3.2	*Explain* the boundaries between the teaching role and other professional roles

Explain the boundaries between the teaching role and other professional roles

- Outline personal and professional boundaries. Personal boundaries would be in relation to your skills and experience relating to your teaching role. Professional boundaries would be defined by your job description and internal line management structures and division of responsibilities (e.g. for quality assurance, coordinating the programme, etc.);
- Describe, using examples the scope and restrictions of your teaching roles referring to the skills and experience you or a hypothetical teacher possesses and how this affects their work with managers and peers (e.g. new teachers may require further training and support, while those with recent industrial experience could provide CPD to peers on that subject area)
- Describe the professional roles a teacher might have at a learning provider, often defined by organisational structures and job descriptions and which could be additional to their teaching role (e.g. Programme Manager, Group Tutor, Lead Internal Verifier or Internal Quality Assurer);
- The focus should be on the limits of the teaching and other professional roles and you need to demonstrate awareness of how these limits can affect your work as a teacher, referring matters to other professionals as needed, which links to assessment criterion 3.3.

Possible response structure:

1. Outline personal and professional boundaries;
2. Describe, using examples and in relation to yourself or a hypothetical teacher (for a hypothetical teacher, you will need to outline length of service,

experience, skills and any additional responsibilities held) the limits of the teaching role and other professional roles;
3. Describe how you or the hypothetical teacher would work with others within the teaching role and in another professional role (e.g. line manager);
4. You should recognise that at some point you may need to refer the matter to others and then explore this aspect further in assessment criterion 3.3.

Assessment criterion 3.3

	Learning outcomes		Assessment criteria
3.	Understand the relationships between teachers and other professionals in education and training	3.3	*Describe* points of referral to meet the individual needs of learners

Describe points of referral to meet the individual needs of learners

- List a range of points of referral, related to individual learner needs, within the learning provider (e.g. to other people or departments, such as Exams, Additional Learning Support, Student Services) and external points of referral (e.g. to external agencies that can offer specialist support or to government agencies, or employers);
- Provide a detailed outline of how the need to refer would be identified, who would be contacted and how, and the manner in which matters would progress. Also outline your role and involvement in this process from referral to any continued contact following referral;
- Outline how such referrals would or should meet the individual needs of the learner.

Possible response structure:

1. List at least three points of referral internally and at least two externally;
2. Provide a detailed outline of the above from identifying the need to refer to referring and any follow-up needed and your role in triggering the referral;
3. Outline how such referrals are likely to meet the needs of the learner.

Printed in Great Britain
by Amazon.co.uk, Ltd.,
Marston Gate.